LARRY BIRD

The Boy From French Lick

By **FRANCINE POPPO RICH**

Illustrated by **ROBERT CASILLA**

Larry Bird: The Boy From French Lick
Published by Blue Marlin Publications

Text copyright © 2009 by Francine Poppo Rich
Illustrations copyright © 2009 by Robert Casilla

Blue Marlin Publications, Ltd.
823 Aberdeen Road, West Bay Shore, NY 11706
www.bluemarlinpubs.com

Printed and bound in China by Regent Publishing Services, Ltd.
October 2009
Job # 091589

Book design & layout by Jude T. Rich

Library of Congress Cataloging-in-Publication Data

Rich, Francine Poppo.
 Larry Bird: the boy from French Lick / By Francine Poppo Rich, illustrated by Robert Casilla.
    p. cm.
 Includes bibliographical references.
 ISBN 978-0-9792918-2-1 (alk. paper) ISBN 978-0-9792918-9-0 (softcover : alk. paper)
 1. Bird, Larry, 1956---Juvenile literature. 2. Basketball players--United States--Biography--Juvenile literature. I. Title.
GV994.B57R54 2009
796.323092--dc22
 [B]

                    2009034581

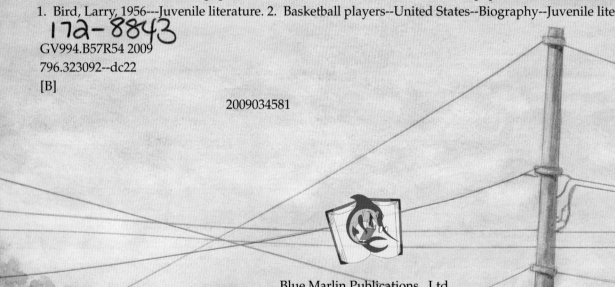

Blue Marlin Publications, Ltd.
823 Aberdeen Road, West Bay Shore, NY 11706
www.bluemarlinpubs.com

For my sister, Marie, my friend for life.
And for my brothers, Michael and John, who took the
time to play *Around the World* with me on our
backyard court.

Francine Poppo Rich

For my son, Rob Casilla Jr., Co-MVP of his basketball
team as a little boy!

Robert Casilla

The little boy from French Lick never cared much about the world beyond the ponds and streams, springs, hills, playground walls, and winding roads that colored his small, country town. He, his four brothers, and his sister never dreamed about faraway places or big cities because his family didn't have a car that could take them to those places. They walked where they wanted to go, and that was far enough. The little boy always liked the things that were right in front of him.

And that little boy certainly never imagined that his basic athletic skills, his determination, and his work ethic were all the ingredients he needed to become one of the best and most respected basketball players who has ever lived. He never dreamed that people would pay to watch him play anything.

French Lick, Indiana is the town where Larry Bird grew up in the 1970s. There are no movie theaters, no McDonald's, no nightclubs, and no malls. But it does have lots of fields and basketball courts, and it is full of decent, hard-working people who all know and care for each other. Larry has never felt more comfortable living any other place.

But Larry's childhood was not perfect. It was hard sometimes. When he was young, his family moved more than 15 times from one rented home to another. Sometimes it was because the rent might be cheaper, and sometimes it was in search of a better furnace to keep the Bird bodies warm. One time, when they moved to a home just down the block, Larry and his sister, Linda, piled beds, a sofa, and everything else they could fit on their little red wagon and pulled the wagon to their new home.

Larry didn't much care what other people might think about that.

Larry was always tall for his age. By the time he was in first grade, he was quite a bit taller than the other children in his class. His first grade teacher, Mrs. Beaty, said, "Because he was so big, he would just knock those little ones down as he ran to his desk. Yet he always helped them up and brushed them off. He was a leader, and the kids loved him."

Larry's father worked as a furniture finisher in a piano factory, and Larry's hard-working mother always had more than one job as a cook or a waitress to help support the family. She would go food shopping on Saturday and would come home with bags and bags of food. But by Thursday, the food would be gone. And there was no money to buy more. So, for the next couple of days, the Bird family would eat just peanut butter and bread. This didn't bother Larry much. It's just the way things were.

While their parents were working, Larry's sister often watched her "rough and tumble" brothers. The Bird boys looked for ways to keep busy and compete against each other in the house. One time, they cut the bottoms out of two coffee cans and nailed the cans to two doors at opposite ends of the hallway. They used a tennis ball and managed to play full court, man–to–man basketball.

Next to one of his homes, Larry had a small baseball field with a concrete wall. As a young boy, he took a rubber or tennis ball to that wall and played for hours. On the weekends, he played baseball there with his two older brothers, Mark and Mike. But they were bigger and stronger, and Larry would have to chase balls and often wouldn't be allowed to bat. Their athletic skills quietly challenged Larry to improve his own.

Even though baseball was actually the sport Larry loved and played the most as a young child, one day, when he was 13, he and his family visited his aunt in Hobart, Indiana (a three–hour drive in a borrowed car—the longest trip he had ever taken with his family). He went for a walk that day and found some older kids playing basketball. They asked him if he wanted to play. When he began sinking shot after shot, his teammates were slapping him on the back, congratulating him, and asking him what team he played on. He wasn't on a team. They were shocked and asked if he could come up to Hobart the following week and play again. Larry smiled and went home, hooked on basketball forever.

Every morning from that point forward, Larry Bird practiced. In ninth grade, he made the high school B team, which meant he could go to all the games. He shot 500 free throws in the gym before school every morning, went to practice after school, and then remained by himself to shoot more. He didn't know how good he was. He just knew he wanted to be better.

Larry watched his brother Mark play in Mark's last game as a Senior. Larry held his breath as Mark made several free throws that helped the Springs Valley Blackhawks win the game. Tears streamed down Larry's face because he couldn't believe how much he loved this game and how proud he was to be Mark's brother. On the bus ride home, Mark, the hero, sat right next to Larry, the little brother. Later, Larry would wear Mark's number, 33, on all his jerseys.

By the time Larry was in 10th grade, he was so interested in playing basketball that he just couldn't get himself to play on the baseball team. He just HAD to play basketball. By now, he was also 6'2" tall and practicing constantly.

Early in the season, though, Larry broke his ankle going for a rebound. He was unable to play most of the season, but he continued to stand every day, propped up on crutches, taking his free throws and passing the ball. During this time, Larry learned something that he believes many players don't understand: that passing is more of an art than scoring. He believes that when a player is open, that player should get the ball. It doesn't matter who scores, as long as it's somebody on your team. And, with crutches in tow, Larry practiced getting the ball to that open player.

IY JASPER

HOLLAND'S HAWKS VISTORIOUS

(body text illegible)

BIRD STEALS THE SHOW

Larry Bird, son of Mr. and Mrs. ...

(body text illegible)

VALLEY

	FG	FT	F	TP
Bird L.J	3	6	2	11
Crock...	4	6	4	10
Clark	9	0	3	20
Ahantur	4	5	0	5
Cluely	6	6	4	0
Hoff	7	0	4	15
Cloth	7	0	1	0
Abrar	0	2	2	5
Bridell	0	0	0	0
Casciro	0	0	0	0
Totals	26	17	14	69

FRIDAY ORDER

	G	UN	6191
WPk			
Webb Hot	6	161	4101

Mihh

	m	AP	P	TP
Down	4	0	4	15
Daoli	4	0	5	14
Dvloll	0	3	4	10
Mocbl	1	0	5	9
Deolich	1	3	5	7
Wochen	1	1	1	7
Holich	0	0	4	8
Hollow	4	1	4	3
Colosn	6	0	1	4
Ewbb				
Totals	11	16	9	44

RINDY BVSKHMHYE

(body text illegible)

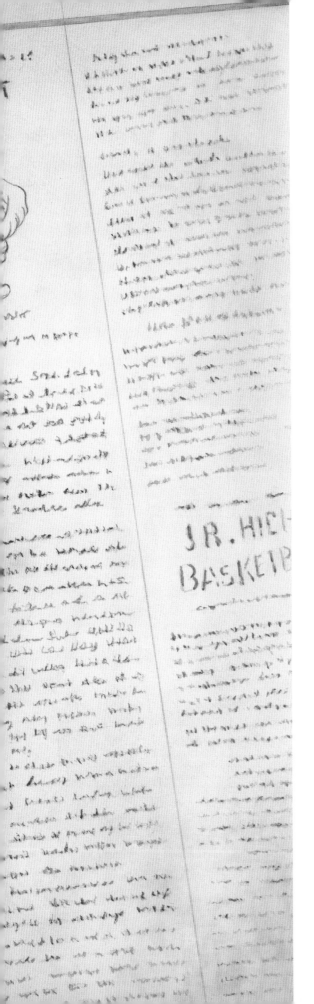

All that crutch-practicing paid off for Larry. By the end of his Sophomore year, his ankle was better, and he played the final seconds of a tournament game. With only four seconds left on the clock, a player fouled Larry. The Blackhawks were down by one point. Larry went to the free throw line. He told himself he was going to make both free throws and win the game. And he did. The next day, the newspaper read, "Bird Steals the Show." After that, Larry spent hours every day drumming up drills to improve his game.

Along the way, a lot of people doubted Larry's abilities. They felt he was slow, he was from a small town, he couldn't jump high, he had trouble playing against the bigger guys, he wasn't good on defense. Some felt he wasn't even a good athlete.

Larry didn't much care what other people might think about him or his abilities as a basketball player. He responded to the doubts of others with a determination and a will to be the best basketball player he could possibly be.

For Larry, basketball was not about fancy moves or high-flying, mind-boggling tricks that would **wow** the crowd. Basketball was about spending hours every day perfecting the fundamental, basic skills of the game. Basketball was about practicing. He listened to everything his high school coach, Jim Jones, told him. He practiced the reverse pivot, playing with both hands, boxing out, getting rebounds, and throwing a hard, one-handed bounce pass. These are the tools of Larry Bird's success—nothing fancy.

Nothing new.

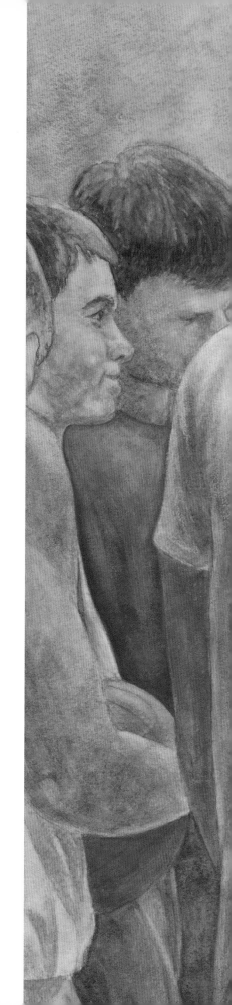

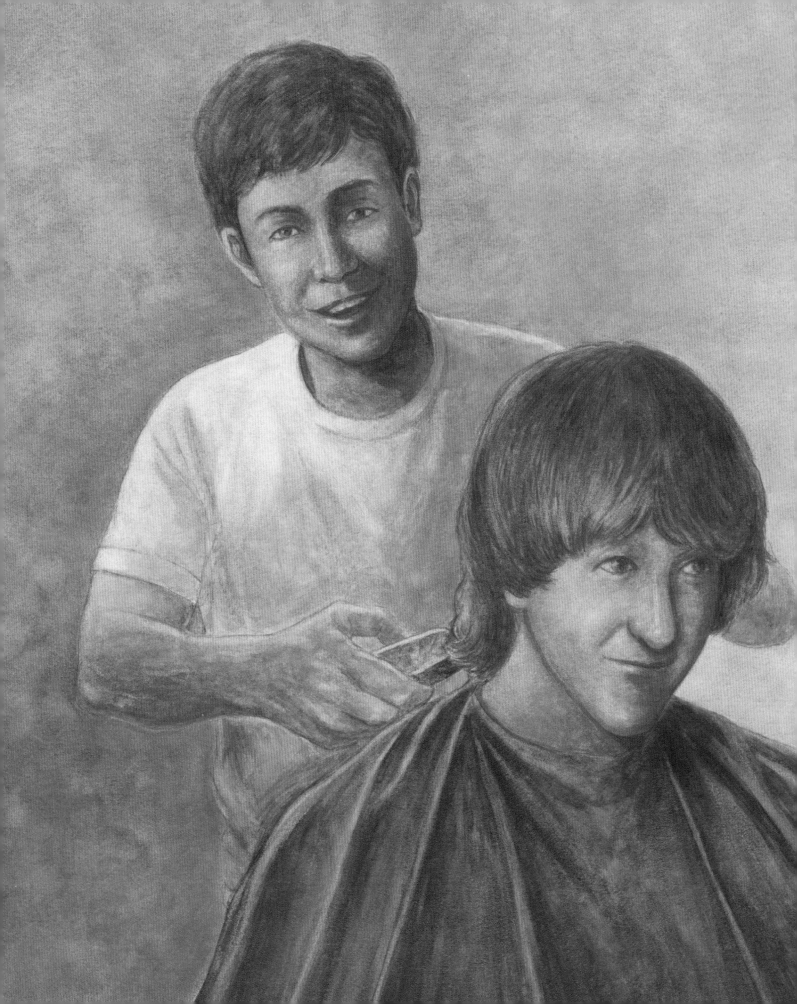

Larry didn't mind working hard because he was learning more about the game he loved. He just kept playing and playing—all day, every day. Most of the time, he didn't even know why. But he did know that he was getting better.

And he was getting taller! By Junior year, Larry was 6'4" tall. During the school year, he met Coach Jones at the school every day at 6 a.m. for free throws. Over the Summer, he practiced on and off with "Jonesie" every day. Some Summer days, Larry played for 14 hours. He was with his coach so much that his coach even cut his hair! On days when he was tired and didn't want to get out of bed, Jonesie would come to his house and wake him up! And when Coach Jones wasn't waking him up, Lizzie Kerns was.

Lizzie Kerns was Larry's grandmother. Because Larry had so many brothers and sisters living in a small home, he often stayed at his grandmother's house, which was also in French Lick. She was Granny, and she was one of the most influential people in young Larry's life. In high school, he would take naps on her floor before his games and sleep at her house for months at a time. When he tried sleeping through his early morning free throws, she would gently come in and say, "Larry, those other boys are down there practicing. You should be down there with them."

And Granny nursed Larry when he was sick. "You lie down and rest, and maybe you'll get to feelin' better," she would say. Then she'd give him an aspirin and a chest rub and put him to sleep. In Granny's home, there was always room for Larry, his troubles, and his basketball schedule. And there was always love.

Through it all, Larry kept growing. By his Senior year, he was 6'7" tall. And he was one of the best basketball players in the state of Indiana. But even the best players sometimes make big mistakes. In a 1974 mid-season game between Larry's Springs Valley Blackhawks and the Loogootee High Lions, Larry broke away, ran down the court, and sank a perfect two-pointer...in the wrong basket! Unfortunately for Larry and the Blackhawks, the Lions won that night—by one point.

But this didn't stop college recruiters from lining up to invite Larry Bird to play on their college teams. They had a hunch that he would never stop improving his game. Still, some college coaches, such as the coach for the University of Kentucky, thought maybe Larry was too slow and would have trouble making shots against bigger players.

Larry didn't much care what anybody thought about him or the future of his game. He loved French Lick. In fact, he would have been perfectly happy to continue with the job he had when he was 18, working for the French Lick Street Department. He loved that job. He loved mowing grass, removing snow, fixing roads, and picking up trash. He worked outside, keeping his town clean, and he loved it. But he also loved playing basketball. And he just couldn't get enough of it.

Larry Bird, at his full height of 6'9", DID go on to become a leader on the Indiana State University's basketball team. He DID go on to play in the NBA for 13 seasons on the Boston Celtics. Those Celtics DID win the NBA championship title in 1981, 1984, and 1986. He WAS voted the most valuable player more than once in the NBA, and he DID win an Olympic Gold Medal in 1992. He even went on to coach the Indiana Pacers, teaching those younger players to focus on the fundamentals—just like he did.

And all of that is very nice, but Larry Bird himself would tell you that he doesn't much care about all that hoopla. He's still the same hick from French Lick.

And darn proud of it.

MORE COOL STUFF ABOUT LARRY BIRD

- While Larry Bird appreciates all the attention he has received as a basketball player, he always was and always will be just a hick from French Lick. That's how he referred to himself in a 1979 press conference, just a few months before he joined the Boston Celtics, where he would play professional basketball for the next 13 years.

- When he was born on December 7, 1956, Larry already weighed 11 pounds, 12 ounces and was 23 inches long. The average weight of a newborn baby is 7.5 pounds, and the average height is 20 inches long. That places Larry well above the height average from the moment he was born!

- At the Boston Garden, whenever the national anthem was played, Larry Bird would stare at the heavens. Lots of people assumed he was studying the Celtics Banners, imagining his name up there someday. But, instead, he was staring at the banner of the retired number 4 from the Bruins' Bobby Orr. Bird stared at that banner so many times, he had the details of the stitching memorized. When Larry Bird played on the Celtics, he had met Orr only once and had never seen him play. But he had heard how great of a hockey player he was and how much Boston admired Orr as a person. Larry revealed this to Orr at a museum dinner celebration in 1988.

- Bob Heaton, a gentleman who played basketball with Larry Bird at Indiana State, recalls a card game at a house he shared with Larry in their Senior year. They were playing poker and blackjack. Larry had lost $2.00. He stood up and excused himself from the game. He had no more money to lose.

- When children imitate Larry Bird, they reach down and rub their hands on the bottoms of their sneakers. Why did Larry do this for so many years, and when did it start? Many people thought he did this to clean and dry his hands. But that's not true. Larry first saw his brothers, Mark and Mike, do this when the high school got new Converse shoes. Their floors were dirty, and they wanted to keep their shoes clean. They would put a little water on their palms, and then they'd wipe the bottoms of their shoes. After they did it, their shoes felt new. Larry started doing it so often, it became habit.

- Larry was always extremely nervous before each game, even as far back as high school. He used to feel so anxious, he thought he was going to vomit. This happened before every game. That's why he always napped the whole afternoon before each game. He would nap for three or four hours. This was his way of dealing with his nervousness. The good thing was that the nervousness always went away the second the game began. This napping tradition continued, even in the NBA.

IMPORTANT DATES IN LARRY BIRD'S BASKETBALL-PLAYING CAREER

1976-1979	Plays for Indiana State University in Terre Haute, Indiana
1979	Signs five-year contract with the Celtics
1980	Named NBA Rookie of the Year
1981	Celtics win NBA Championship, defeating Houston Rockets, 4-2
1982	Named All-Star Game MVP
1983	Signs seven-year contract with the Boston Celtics
1984	Celtics win NBA Championship against the Lakers, 4-2. Lakers are led by Magic Johnson.
1984	Named League MVP
1985	Named League MVP
1986	Named League MVP and Play-off MVP
1986	Celtics win NBA Championship against Houston Rockets, 4-2
1984, 85, 87, and 90	Holds free throw shooting title
1992	Wins Olympic Gold Medal for the USA Dream Team

BIBLIOGRAPHY

Quotes

"Because he was so big...the kids loved him." Corn. *Basketball's Magnificent Bird: The Larry Bird Story*, p.5.

"Larry, those other boys...down there with them." Bird. *Drive*, p.17

"You lie down...feelin' better." *Basketball's Magnificent Bird: The Larry Bird Story*, p.13.

Books

Bird, Larry with Jackie MacMullan. *Bird Watching*. New York: Warner Books, 1999.

Bird, Larry with Bob Ryan. *Drive*. New York: Doubleday, 1989.

Bird, Larry with John Bischoff. *Bird on Basketball: How-to Strategies From the Great Celtics Champion*. Reading, MA: Perseus Books, 1983 and 1986.

Corn, Frederick Lynn. *Basketball's Magnificent Bird: The Larry Bird Story*. New York: Random House, 1982.

Larry Bird: An Indiana Legend Presented by...The Indianapolis Star The Indianapolis News. Champaign, IL: Sports Publishing, Inc., 1999.

Smith, L Virginia. *Larry Bird: From Valley Hick to Boston Celtic*. Indiana: L. Virginia Smith, 1982.

Articles

I read hundreds of newspaper and magazine articles. Most of these pull information from the sources listed above. Below is a partial list of some great articles that shed light on additional aspects of Larry Bird's life.

Courier Journal: January 28, 1979 and June 30, 1998
Current Biography, v43 no6: June 1982
The Indianapolis Star On-line Library Factfiles
New York Times: March 26, 1979
Sports Illustrated: November 28, 1977; January 23, 1978; November 9, 1981; and March 21, 1988
Springs Valley Herald: January 13, 1972; August 12, 19, and 26, 1992; October 14, 1998
Time: March 18, 1985
Times-Mail: September 28 and 29, 1998

How French Lick got its name: French Lick and the nearby town of West Baden Springs are in a valley located in the heart of the Hoosier National Forest. There are many mineral water springs found here that have attracted people from all over the world for more than two hundred years. The free-flowing spring water left a residue of salt on the rocks surrounding the springs. Initially, French Fur Traders, Missionaries, and Adventurers discovered what they considered healing powers in the springs, along with the plentiful supply of salt. The deer, bear, and buffalo came to the springs to lick the salt off the rocks. Thus, the area came to be called French Lick.